POLAR BEARS!
AN ANIMAL ENCYCLOPEDIA FOR KIDS (BEAR KINGDOM)
CHILDREN'S BIOLOGICAL SCIENCE OF BEARS BOOKS

PRODIGYWIZARD
BOOKS

Are you familiar with Polar Bears? Have you seen one? Lets learn some interesting facts about Polar Bears!

Polar bears are also known scientifically as "ursus maritimus".

It is estimated
that there are
almost 2000
polar bears
in the wild.

Polar bears are clothed in hollow fluffy transparent fur but their skin is black. Their fur blends with their snowy surroundings.

Their fur appears white and reflects light. Their fur traps the sun's heat and keeps them warm.

They are the largest meat eaters or carnivores that live on land. These bears are also so strong that they can kill their prey by just one blow of their paw!

Polar bears eat seals as their primary diet. That is why they are found near the sea most of the time.

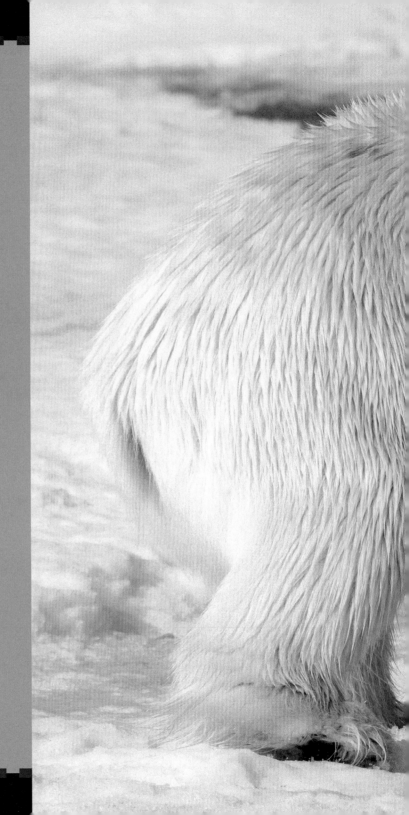

To hunt seals, polar bears use sea ice as a platform.

Having a strong sense of smell, polar bears are capable of smelling seals at a distance of 1 mile away.

Polar bears have rough-surfaced paw pads which prevent them from slipping off the icy surface.

Male polar bears can weigh up to 1500 pounds. While the females are just the half of the male's weight.

Polar bears conserve warmth by curling up and covering their nose or muzzle with their paws.

On land, polar bears can move up to 25 miles per hour. While in water, they can swim 6 miles per hour. Polar bears have oily fur which is water repellent.

Female polar bears can have babies starting at 4 - 5 years of age. The mother bears will not hibernate but will stay and live in dens while they take care of their young.

Polar bears slow down their metabolism while they are still looking for their next meal. Their fat reserves make this possible.

Polar bear cubs strictly follow rules and form habits. They learn to keep moving. If their mother is not there because she is looking for food, if they stayed still they would freeze.

Polar bears are part of our most precious environment. They need to be admired and protected.

But it is sad to note that their main predators are humans. Man made pollutions also cause their death. Global warming is also a threat to their existence.

We can all do something to help. In our own little way we can take steps to improve the environment and protect the Polar Bears.

Made in the USA
San Bernardino, CA
31 March 2018